behind the news | **GLOBAL BUSINESS**:
who benefits?

DAVID DOWNING

www.heinemann.co.uk/library

Visit our website to find out more information about Heinemann Library books.

To order:
☎ Phone 44 (0) 1865 888112
📄 Send a fax to 44 (0) 1865 314091
💻 Visit the Heinemann bookshop at www.heinemann.co.uk/library to browse our catalogue and order online.

First published in Great Britain by Heinemann Library, Halley Court, Jordan Hill, Oxford OX2 8EJ, part of Harcourt Education.

Heinemann Library is a registered trademark of Harcourt Education Ltd.

Editorial: Andrew Farrow and Richard Woodham
Design: David Poole and Kamae Design
Picture Research: Ruth Blair and Natalie Gray
Production: Huseyin Sami

Originated by Modern Age
Printed and bound in China by South China Printing Company

10-digit ISBN 0 431 11472 2
13-digit ISBN 978 0 431 11472 9
11 10 09 08 07
10 9 8 7 6 5 4 3 2 1

British Library Cataloguing in Publication Data
Downing, David
Global business: who benefits?. - (Behind the news)
337
A full catalogue record for this book is available from the British Library.

Acknowledgements
The publishers would like to thank the following for permission to reproduce photographs:
Alamy pp. 9 (Image Source), 32 (Sue Cunningham Photographic), 35 (Ashley Cooper), 46 (Steven May), 47 (Edward Parker); Corbis pp. 5 (Mike Alquinto/Epa), 7 (Macduff Everton), 10 (Louie Psihoyos), 16 (Frederik Brent), 17 (Punit Paranjpe/ Reuters), 19 (Stephen Jaffe/Imf), 21 (Jack Kurtz/Zuma), 23 (Jagadeesh Nv/ Reuters), 24 (Robert Wallis), 30 (Reuters), 37 (Nik Wheeler), 42 (Reuters), 45 (Reuters); EMPICS pp. 4 (AP), 14 (AP), 15 (AP), 27 (AP), 48 (AP), 49 (AP); Fairtrade International p. 46 (www.transfairusa.org); Getty Images pp. 11 (CNN), 18, 29, 39 (AFP), 41; Harcourt Education p. 40; Impact p. 25 (Mark Henley); Panos pp. 12 (Sven Torfinn), 34 (Mark Henley); Still Pictures p. 13 (C.Garroni Parisi); Superstock p. 22 (Emmanuel Faure); Topfoto p. 31 (Imageworks).

Cover photograph reproduced with permission of Getty Images (Robert Nickelsberg).

The author and Publishers gratefully acknowledge the publications from which the longer written sources in the book are drawn. In some cases the wording or sentence structure has been simplified to make the material appropriate for a school readership:

BBC Information Service pp.5, 20, 31, 40; *Business Asia* p.24; CNN.com p.30; the *Ecologist* (www.theecologist.org) pp.8, 35; the *Independent* pp.12, 13, 17, 43; the *New Internationalist* pp.20, 27; the *Observer* p.44; *Time* magazine p.36.

CONTENTS

Any words appearing in the text in bold, **like this**, are explained in the glossary.

Agribusiness

In recent times one of the fastest-growing global businesses has been the global agricultural business (agribusiness, for short). Agribusiness companies have been busy developing new seeds for crops. They have used the most modern **biotechnological** ideas and techniques to make seeds that are more resistant to pests and diseases. These **genetically modified (GM)** seeds produce more food per plant than "natural" seeds.

In a world in which around a billion people regularly go hungry, these seeds might seem like the answer to a huge problem. You would think that the global businesses that carry them to all parts of the world would always be welcome. President George W. Bush of the United States certainly thought so. According to a report on the White House website, he told the American Biotechnology industry's 2003 convention: "Through the work of scientists in your field, many farmers in developed nations are able to grow crops with high resistance to drought and pests and disease, and to produce far greater yields per acre . . . we should encourage the spread of safe, effective biotechnology to win the fight against global hunger."

President Bush did recognize that there was some opposition to the genetic modification of seeds: "'Acting on unfounded, unscientific fears, many European governments have blocked the import of all new biotech crops,' Mr Bush said. 'Because of these artificial obstacles, many African nations avoid investing in biotechnology, worried that their products will be shut out of important European markets. For the sake of a continent threatened by famine, I urge the European governments to end their opposition to biotechnology.'"

According to this report, President Bush offered no reason for the European opposition. He merely claimed that it was based on "unfounded, unscientific fears".

The impressive headquarters of Germany's Frankfurt-based Deutsche Bank are a sign of corporate power and influence.

Global business has helped to bring new technology to the developing world. Do you think this is a positive or negative impact of global business?

A different view

Obviously, the European governments believed that they had good reasons for blocking the import of GM seeds and crops. Many European scientists, and a large proportion of the continent's people, feared that these products posed a threat to their health and environment.

Europe was not the only opponent of the new technology. Three years earlier, BBC News online carried the following story: "Thousands of farmers and environmental activists have rallied in the southern Indian city of Bangalore to protest against the development of genetically modified crops . . . The activists say they want to stop foreign **multinational** companies selling the seeds in Asian markets . . . The meeting heard harrowing accounts of farmers who had committed suicide because of crop failures allegedly caused by genetically modified seeds and fake pesticides . . . The leading Indian environmentalist, Vandana Shiva, told the farmers that GM seeds had ruined India's traditional seed varieties and reduced yields." GM crops were clearly not the answer for everyone, and global businesses providing GM seeds were not always welcome.

Why are the reports above so different? Which story is more accurate, and how can we tell?

A new idea?

At first sight, global business seems simple to define – it is all those economic activities that are international in scope. Defined in this way it seems far from new. Travellers on the ancient Silk Road who carried goods between China and Europe were carrying out a type of global business. British ships that carried slaves from Africa to America in the 18th century were part of an international trading system. The oil industry of the 20th century quickly grew to cover the entire world. Global business, in its simplest form, has been with us for a long time.

A change of scale

Over the last couple of decades there have been three developments that have changed the scale, scope, and character of global business.

- A series of technological advances – in telecommunications, computing, and transport – have made it much quicker and easier to move information, goods, and services around the world.
- The collapse of **communism** in the late 1980s opened up markets that had previously been closed. This allowed **free enterprise capitalism** to become a truly global system.
- There has been an almost worldwide acceptance of the belief that global business can benefit everyone. The triumph of Western capitalism over Soviet communism was seen as a victory for the free enterprise system and its values. It was assumed that what had worked for the West would now work for the world as a whole. The growth of global business has therefore been actively encouraged not only by businesses, but also by politicians and the media.

Most global business is done by privately owned companies or **corporations**. Over the last few decades many of these corporations have grown much larger. Some have bigger budgets than the countries they do business in. Some, for example Nike or Coca-Cola, have become global brand names that are recognized all over the world. These giant, **transnational** corporations are usually based in one country, but operate in many different countries. They work globally, and are able to move their operations from one country to another in search of higher profits.

The old global business was mostly restricted to trade in raw materials and manufactured goods. Modern innovations such as the Internet and satellite phones have made possible a global trade in financial and other services. Over the last 15 years most countries have changed their laws to allow the

Global brands reach all corners of the world. A branch of the US coffee bar chain Starbucks has been opened inside Forbidden City in Beijing, China.

free movement of money across borders. Bankers also work globally, and they move their money around in search of the best investments and highest **interest** rates.

This ability to shift jobs and money across borders has made it much harder for some governments to control their own **economies**. In some cases, corporations have become more powerful than governments.

A mixed blessing?

Global business has been a mixed blessing. Even Pascal Lamy, the head of the **World Trade Organization (WTO)**, admits that world trade "has good sides and bad sides". According to an article in the *Independent* in November 2005, Lamy said, "we have to acknowledge that the reshuffling it [global business] creates in the social fabric has to be coped with."

Some countries, groups, and individuals have benefited from global business, while others have suffered. Many have done both. A young couple in a rich Western city, for example, might enjoy a rising standard of living, cheaper electronic goods, and a wider choice of foods. At the same time they might find that their parents are getting a smaller pension as corporations put profits before looking after their employees. They may also see their children suffer as businesses put growth before caring for the planet.

For and against

Newspaper articles and TV news items that support the rise of global business are quite easy to find. Articles that are fiercely against global business are harder to find in mainstream media, but are quite common in **environmentalist** publications. Below are extracts from articles that seem to be for and against global business. They might seem to contradict each other, but they are really telling different parts of the same story.

In February 2004 the *Northwest Pennsylvania Business Journal* reported how a US furniture maker in Pennsylvania began to work with the Chinese market in 2001. The company started to sell its furniture parts to Chinese companies, which then assembled furniture for the company. Its international sales director said, "We saw the trend of low-cost Chinese-made furniture and we decided to take advantage of it." Many newspapers have explained how world trade allowed China and India, the world's two most populous nations, to grow by 9 and 8 per cent in 2005. Both the Chinese workers and US consumers have benefited from the opening up of world trade.

The following appeared in the May/June edition of the *Ecologist*:
"Today, western consumer conformity [sameness] is descending on the less-industrialised parts of the world like an avalanche. 'Development' brings tourism, western films and products and, more recently, satellite television to the remotest parts of the earth. All provide overwhelming images of luxury and power. Adverts and action films give the impression that everyone in the West is rich, beautiful and brave, and leads a life filled with excitement and glamour . . . People are not aware of the negative social or psychological aspects of Western life so familiar to us: the stress, the loneliness, the fear of growing old, the rise in clinical depression and other 'industrial diseases' like cancer, stroke, diabetes and heart problems. Nor do they see the environmental decay, rising crime, poverty, homelessness and unemployment. While they know their own culture inside out, including all of its limitations and imperfections, they see only a glossy, exaggerated side of life in the West."

How do we, as individuals, form our opinions about global business? Where do we get our facts? Some of us, or some of our relations, probably work for a global business. All of us buy or consume products of global business, so we do have some direct knowledge. Yet, we only see a tiny part of the picture. The label in our T-shirt tells us where it was made, but it doesn't tell us how the cotton growers or the T-shirt makers were treated. Where, then, do we turn for the whole picture? Mostly, we turn to the media.

Newspapers are just one part of the modern media. Today, the public can choose from a huge range of national and international newspapers.

Rupert Murdoch is the classic global businessman. The Australian media tycoon now owns important newspapers and television channels across the world.

Opinions in journalism

Global business often appears in works of fiction, for example in novels and films, and there are many non-fiction works that explore the subject. Most people, however, form their opinions about global business from the news and current affairs media. The views expressed in these media are many and varied, but all tend to be **biased**.

A situation where everything is working normally is not usually thought of as newsworthy. Surprises or conflicts are usually considered "news". This has the effect of exaggerating the negative aspects of whatever is being reported – and global business is no exception. An international oil company that keeps its workers and customers satisfied is not news. An international oil company caught up in a dispute with environmentalists most definitely is news. Global business tends to get mentioned in the news when something bad has happened.

The media, of course, have to be aware of what is going on. Media companies now have journalists and correspondents who specialize in reporting globalization issues such as protests and environmental concerns.

Whose opinions?

How the media report events depends on the opinions and biases of those involved. Editors and journalists have their own opinions and biases, which will affect their coverage of stories. The owners of the various media will also have opinions and biases, and they will generally expect their television stations and newspapers to reflect them. Owners can hire and fire their staff, so it is the owners' opinions and biases that usually matter the most. Not surprisingly, the owners usually support free enterprise capitalism, which made them wealthy enough to buy a newspaper or TV station.

An untold story

Business reporting is usually kept separate from political reporting. Newspapers have their own business pages, and TV and radio news programmes have their own business slots. However, most political decisions are also economic decisions, and vice versa. If a government decides to upgrade its country's health care facilities the whole economy will be affected. If a global business decides to expand its operations, the changes in employment will have a political impact. Yet the first story will usually feature in the political pages. The second, if it appears at all, will be found in the business section.

In general, there is little coverage of global business in the mainstream media. Business news seems aimed at people in business, and not at the general public. This may be because editors and journalists feel that most business stories are not newsworthy. They may also believe that the general public has little interest or understanding of the subject. Whatever the reason, people are given considerably less information about business developments than they are about political developments. Unlike politicians, business people are rarely asked to explain or defend their actions.

A political story such as an event in the War on Terror is more likely to make media headlines than a business story. This "breaking news" was about the al-Qaeda leader Osama bin Laden.

Protests in Hong Kong

The World Trade Organization meeting in Hong Kong in December 2005 concentrated on global business. Despite the failure to reach agreement on the main issues dividing richer and poorer countries, much of the Western media was keen to stress the benefits of global business.

The *Independent* reported that: "To understand what is happening in Hong Kong – and why it does really matter – don't focus on the rows . . . The talks matter because they are part of a continuing process that has been going on for more than half a century to rid the world of the restrictions that wrecked the world economy in the first half of the last century."

A Shell logo appears here on the side of a hut in Nigeria's Niger delta. There is no indication here that the region's oil wealth has benefited the local inhabitants.

Workers strung out across a tea plantation in the Indian state of Kerala. Their wages represent a tiny percentage of the profits made from the tea they pick.

The same newspaper's **editorial**, however, was more critical: " The leaders of the world's richest nations are all in favour of **free trade**. But only when it suits them. In sectors such as manufacturing and services, the great trading blocs of Europe, America and Asia are generally happy to allow the unimpeded exchange of goods and skills across national borders. But there is a shameful exception: agriculture. Here, free trade simply does not exist. For a variety of political and cultural reasons, Europe, the US and Japan **subsidize** their farmers and refuse to open their **domestic market** properly to produce from the developing world. It is this agricultural **protectionism** – more than perhaps any other single factor – that keeps those in the most deprived regions of the world in poverty."

Other media also chose to report criticisms of the WTO meeting. The news website www.usnewswire.com, for example, quoted Adriano Campolina Soares, director of ActionAid Americas: " This summit is a failure. It has delivered only paltry [worthless] reductions in subsidies, and has gone into dangerous terrain [ground] on the **privatization** of basic services such as water and healthcare. Poor farmers have also received no protection from highly subsidized foreign produce. Even if their governments can live with this outcome, it is poor people who will pay the ultimate price."

Global expansion

Business companies exist to make money for their owners by selling goods and services. Until recently most businesses preferred to operate inside their own country. This was because setting up and running **subsidiaries** (branches) in foreign countries was difficult. Transporting goods, transferring money, and communicating with headquarters were all costly and time-consuming. As these things grew cheaper, simpler, and quicker, companies realized they could sell more goods or services by operating abroad. In theory, these companies could come from anywhere. In practice, nearly all transnational companies come from wealthy, developed countries.

Companies have many ways of expanding their operations. A German chocolate company, for example, could close down a factory in Germany and open a new one in a poorer country where the wages are much lower. If it already got its raw cocoa from Ghana in Africa, it would probably choose to set up its new factory there. The same company could also expand by buying the cocoa farms that supply the factory, the aeroplanes and lorries that move the chocolate to shops, or the shops themselves.

These forms of global expansion offer benefits to companies. Lower costs mean higher profits. Successful companies have invested some of their profits in buying up other companies. They have tightened their grip on one corner of their market or expanded into other areas. Companies have grown into huge corporations. This pattern has been repeated across the world in many industries. World trade has grown, and so have corporate profits.

A Honda car assembly plant just outside the Indian capital Delhi. The Japanese company has moved production to India because labour and other costs are cheaper.

Vietnamese workers at a Nike factory in Ho Chi Minh City put the finishing touches to a batch of athletic shoes. The shoes will be sold in shops around the world.

The power of transnational corporations

Imagine it is around 1975. The toy division of a US corporation has always made its toys at its US factory. Its costs, by world standards, are high. The local **trade union** has always insisted on reasonable wages, a 40-hour week, and **health benefits** for the workforce. If the management refuses any of these things, then the workers will refuse to work. In addition, the government has recently introduced new regulations concerning waste disposal and pollution. These will cost the corporation a lot of money.

Move on 10 to 15 years, and things have changed. The corporation can cut costs and increase profits by shifting production to a poorer country. It tells its US workers that they have a choice: they can either accept lower wages, longer hours, and fewer benefits or see their jobs moved to a Central American country such as Honduras. Workers in Honduras will be willing to work for less money and no benefits.

In Honduras, meanwhile, the corporation's representatives explain the situation to the local politicians. The politicians agree to waive (ignore) business taxes and **environmental regulations** because the factory will provide jobs. If they don't agree, the corporation can find another country that will.

The corporation will increase its profits in both cases. In both countries, the corporation has the stronger position. Many corporations do not behave as ruthlessly as this fictional example, but most have the power to do so if they wish. Only the most powerful governments, international organizations, and **mass campaigning movements** can take on the major corporations with any hope of success.

Seeking an advantage

National governments sometimes intervene to protect the jobs of their own people. They do this by giving extra money – **subsidies** – to their own businesses. This enables businesses to pay higher costs and still remain competitive.

Subsidies for farmers

The **European Union (EU)**, for example, supports its farmers with subsidies. This allows the farmers to sell their produce at less than its real cost, and compete successfully with farmers from poorer countries who have no such help. The United States does the same for its cotton farmers giving them approximately US$3.4billion (£2 billion) a year in subsidies. This financial help allows US farmers to sell their cotton at a cheaper price than their overseas competitors. As a result the United States is now the world's biggest exporter of cotton.

The Hong Kong Stock Exchange is part of a global network of exchanges where shares in companies are traded. Corporations and governments can raise huge sums of money by issuing shares and bonds there.

Many banking companies provide financial services internationally. This branch of a western bank is in Kenya, but the bank's name and products would be familiar to people in many countries around the world.

Rich vs. poor

Subsidies give richer countries an advantage in the global marketplace. For the cotton farmers of small African countries – whose entire **GDP** is smaller than the subsidy received by US cotton farmers – the consequences can be devastating. Take one farmer from Burkina Faso, for example: "Seydou, dressed in a ripped T-shirt that hangs off his shoulders, looks blank when questioned about the effect of United States subsidies on his only source of income, cotton farming. 'I don't know about cotton prices in the US but I know cotton prices have fallen here in Burkina Faso' he says solemnly . . . In front of Seydou's mud house, a pile of bright-white cotton sits drying in the glaring sun. Inside the walls are bare, except for a single cross . . .
'I cannot afford to buy things because cotton prices keep fluctuating. I know cotton grows well here but prices are down so I cannot send my youngest son to school. This makes me sad. I know his only chance of a good future is school.'" This quote comes from the *Independent* newspaper from December 2005.

Help and hindrance

Transnational corporations are very powerful, and promise economic growth. Governments have therefore usually tried to help rather than hinder them. Governments have many ways of doing this. They can reduce the taxes that corporations and their managers have to pay. They can remove rules and regulations that make it more difficult for the corporations to operate. They can pass laws that make it harder for trade unions to defend workers' wages and benefits. They can campaign in the various international organizations for more freedom of movement across borders of goods, money, and services. All of these things are done to create an environment that is "corporate-friendly".

Some global business is directly supported by governments. Many western governments help their defence industries at international exhibitions, like this one.

International organizations

There are three major international organizations that deal with global business: the **International Monetary Fund (IMF)**, the **World Bank**, and the World Trade Organization (WTO). The IMF and World Bank began operating in 1946.

The IMF was set up to maintain international economic stability. It was supposed to keep a careful eye on the movement of money from country to country, and to help countries that got into financial difficulty. Many of the poorer countries did get into difficulty by borrowing large sums of money that they then found they were unable to pay back (see box on page 20).

International
Monetary Fund
manager Oure
Cassoni visits
a refugee camp
in Chad.

The World Bank was supposed to lend money to governments – particularly those of poorer countries – for long-term development projects such as road networks and large dams. The third organization, the WTO, began operating in 1995 to take the place of the **General Agreement on Tariffs and Trade (GATT)**. GATT was set up to reduce world **trade barriers**, and much progress was made during the inter-governmental negotiations that took place between 1947 and 1993. Since 1995 the WTO has attempted to free up world trade still further.

The IMF and World Bank are not open, **democratic** organizations. They are effectively controlled by the richer countries of the world, and by the United States in particular. Power is more widely shared in the WTO, but richer countries have traditionally dominated it. All three organizations have followed "corporate-friendly" policies. When asked to help a country in difficulty the IMF and World Bank only agree to do so on certain conditions. The country's government has almost always been told to improve its financial situation by spending less on things such as health and education, and by selling off government-owned businesses such as water and electricity companies. Transnational corporations usually buy these businesses from governments. Through the WTO richer countries have successfully removed trade barriers that their own corporations find most restrictive.

Conflicting reports on the IMF

In the mainstream media the IMF, World Bank, and WTO – like global business as whole – are rarely challenged. This report from BBC News online is fairly typical: "The International Monetary Fund has approved a $4.8bn (£2.8bn) plan to cancel the debts of 20 of the world's poorest countries . . . Among the countries benefiting are Benin, Bolivia, Burkina Faso, Cambodia, Ethiopia, Ghana, Guyana, Mali, Nicaragua, Niger, Rwanda and Tanzania. Most of them have qualified for the IMF debt relief by undertaking economic reforms and taking steps to reduce corruption."

The BBC report does not mention what these "economic reforms" are. The article below comes from the March 2004 edition of the *New Internationalist*. It goes into more detail, and is far more critical: "The IMF record in restoring countries to rude [vigorous] financial health is so appalling that were it a private corporation selling its advice on the open market it would long ago have gone bust. Its advice to any finance minister is exactly the same, whatever the international economic climate, whatever the local market circumstances: cut government spending; privatize your public-sector organizations; remove subsidies of all kinds; open up your economy to transnational finance and corporations."

Although most governments have tended to encourage global business and corporations, governments of both richer and poorer countries have, at times, tried to restrain them. In poorer countries the corporations have sometimes gone too far. They have exploited cheap labour and done environmental damage, while offering very little to the country concerned. In such situations, local governments have sometimes chosen – or sometimes been forced – to side with their own angry people against the corporations. Both the United States and the European Union have intervened to check the free run of global business. They are large and powerful enough to partially restrain the corporations. They rarely do so, however, because in most cases they believe that unrestrained global business benefits their own economies.

THE DEBT PROBLEM

In the 1960s and 1970s many of the poorer countries of the world borrowed large sums of money from wealthy countries to finance development projects. A variety of circumstances including rising oil prices, declining **export revenue**, and government corruption and incompetence made it difficult for many countries to pay these loans back. This financial difficulty was in nobody's long-term interest, and since the 1980s there has been a growing – and partially successful – international campaign for cancellation or reduction of these debts.

Putting on a good face

In some cases individual corporations have been publicly accused of bad or irresponsible behaviour, and people have been asked not to buy their products. These protests are not always highly effective, but corporations do take them seriously. Corporations spend large amounts of money on creating a good image for themselves. For example, the US oil corporation ExxonMobil supports the Save The Tiger Fund by donating US$1 million every year. Big oil companies have all been criticized over the years for damaging the environment. ExxonMobil is obviously keen to show the public that it shares their environmental concerns, and that it behaves in an environmentally responsible manner.

Employees of the America West airline company protest against a merger that threatens their jobs. Despite their power, huge corporations can still be restrained or influenced by the pressure of public opinion.

The impact of global business

The growth of global business has had implications for most areas of human life. Most obviously, it has had economic implications. It has changed who makes what, who is employed, and how well people and countries are doing economically. Global business also has profound implications for politics, the environment, culture, health, and education.

The changes associated with global business have not affected everyone in the same way. Some countries have done much better than others. Some groups of people within each country have done better than others. Some have benefited and some have suffered: there have been winners and losers.

In rich countries

Global business has meant more business for richer countries. They have more trade and more products. Their economies have grown even stronger, and, generally speaking, their people's standard of living has continued to rise. The range of products has expanded, and many have become cheaper. Things such as personal computers and foreign holidays – both of which were considered luxuries only 20 years ago – are now taken for granted by many families.

"Going out of business" is a common sign in many towns and cities. While some people have benefited enormously from global business, it has also resulted in the loss of many jobs in richer countries. High unemployment in some areas has put pressure on welfare systems.

Indian graduates queue for job interviews outside a newly established software company in the southern city of Bangalore. These workers will be paid less than people doing the same job in richer countries.

Not everyone has been so fortunate. Workers in businesses that moved their production to poorer countries have lost their jobs. Where these businesses were grouped into old industrial regions, large pockets of high unemployment and relative poverty have appeared. At the same time, the need to be competitive on the global market has led the governments of most rich countries to cut spending on **welfare** and health. In the United States, for example, funding for community health projects has been severely cut back in recent years. As a result of these developments, a **significant minority** in richer countries have missed out on the benefits of global business.

While most people are better off, another significant minority have seen a spectacular rise in their personal wealth. The gap between those at the very top of the economic pile and those at the very bottom has widened in all of the richer countries of the world.

This mother and child in a Delhi slum have been untouched by the growth of India's economy.

In poor countries

While few people dispute that global business has made rich countries even richer, opinions are divided about its economic effect on poorer countries.

In March 2005, Michael Preiss reported in *Business Asia* that: "India is firmly emerging from the shadows of history into the glare of a globalised world. India's **Congress**-led government has the ambitious goal of sustained annual GDP growth of 7 per cent to 8 per cent and a doubling of **per capita income** over the next ten years, the result of which will lift millions of people out of poverty and transform the country beyond recognition."

Some Indians, however, thought differently. Polls have suggested that a majority of Indians believe their standard of living has fallen after 5 years of economic reform. Many poor Indians believe that global business has made a small number of people wealthier, but made the poor even poorer. There have been many large protests by communities against the large corporations, who had been welcomed into the country by a government keen for foreign investment.

Again, this shows two sides of the same story. For many people in poorer countries global business has meant more, and better, jobs than they had before. They can earn more money and learn new skills. Their countries' transport and communication systems have been improved, and their cities have new airports, skyscrapers, and Internet cafes. There is a wider choice of goods to buy: from clothes to mobile phones. People can, if they wish, enjoy

Western junk food, television programmes, and music. They have become an essential part of the global economy.

Most of these developments, however, have been in cities. Millions of people have migrated from the countryside to take the new jobs. As there are almost always more migrants than jobs, the companies are able to keep wages low. Many of those who do find work send part of their pay back to their families in the countryside. Those who cannot find work – and many of those that do – can only afford to live in houses without running water or electricity.

The amount of debt that many poorer countries are in greatly affects the local quality of life. The loan interest payments consume a large slice of what little money these countries have. Many governments have been forced to spend less on health, education, and welfare.

The widening gap

As in rich countries, the gap between the top and bottom earners in poor countries has widened over the last 20 years. The local **elites** have benefited enormously from global business. Almost all of the capital cities in poor countries have zones of luxury housing, with troops or police permanently deployed to keep the poor out.

In poor countries global business has only benefited a minority. In countries with huge populations, such as India and China, this minority may be several hundred million strong, but it is still a minority. The spectacular transformation of cities such as Shanghai and Chennai is much more obvious than the lack of change in thousands of villages. India and China are the "success" stories. As far as Africa is concerned, global business has been an economic catastrophe. Over the last 20 years an already poor continent has grown even poorer.

Impressive apartment blocks for the rich overshadow the slums of the poor here in Jakarta, Indonesia.

The end of democracy?

"The World Trade Organization has plans to replace that outmoded political idea: **democracy**." This was how an article in the *Observer* newspaper in 2001 began. What was the story behind this opening line? Could it be true that the World Trade Organization was trying to replace democracy?

Supporters of free enterprise capitalism and free trade have traditionally claimed that economic freedom – leaving business free to accumulate wealth in whatever ways come naturally – actually encourages political freedom and democracy. Supporters of global business claim that they are helping to spread freedom and democracy around the world. According to the website www.useu.be, the United States Mission to the European Union certainly believes that this is case: "A recent survey of twelve African nations that have introduced democratic and **market reforms** over the last decade revealed that support for democracy is widespread. Even as a significant proportion cited their dissatisfaction with their country's economy, the bottom line was that the respondents expected democracy to improve their **socio-economic** well-being. Plainly, the people of these nations believe as we do that political and economic reforms are two sides of the same coin."

Opponents of global business dispute such claims. As global business has become more powerful, they argue, so governments have become weaker. While national governments used to have more economic power than the largest businesses, this is often no longer the case.

Governments used to be able to control the flow of goods, money, and services that crossed their borders, but new global trade rules now prevent them from doing so. National economies have become so entangled with the wider global economy that national governments can hardly make a move without permission from the transnational corporations and international economic organizations. A government that wishes to protect an ailing industry and its workers now finds it much more difficult to do so. In the past the government would have taken steps to limit similar imports from abroad – giving the industry a chance to keep its domestic market. Today's trade rules generally outlaw such practices.

Is it worth voting?

The power of global business obviously has serious consequences for national democracies. If the real decisions are being taken by unelected corporate chiefs and international institutions then why bother voting for national governments? Paul Kingsnorth of the *New Internationalist* came to the following conclusion in November 2004: "The global free market and systems of democracy are not, as we are told from all sides, complementary: they are antagonistic. You can have one but, it seems, you cannot have the other. The spread of the free market does not aid the spread of a free politics. Quite the opposite: it eats democracy for breakfast . . . For it is demonstrably true that, as the power of the market has eaten away at the power of the people, politicians, like politics itself, have changed. In virtually every democracy on Earth, '**Right**' and '**left**' have become almost meaningless terms. Whoever you vote for, they will have to keep the markets happy or see their economy crushed. Whatever and whoever you vote for, you will get **neo-liberalism**."

Supporters of Ukraine's pro-democracy "Orange Revolution" listen to a speech in Kiev's Independence Square.

Political implications for rich countries

The weakening of democracy is most marked in rich countries. The number of people voting in recent years has declined in most countries, and one important reason for this is the widespread feeling that it doesn't change anything. People know that the success of their national economy depends on global business, and that their government has to play by global business rules. They know that maintaining their own prosperity means keeping their own country competitive.

This has had political consequences. **Right-wing** governments – for example those led by Ronald Reagan in the United States (1981–1989) and Margaret Thatcher in the United Kingdom (1979–1990) – have always had policies that help business. By the 1990s even **left-wing** governments – for example those led by Tony Blair in the United Kingdom after 1997 and Gerhard Schröder in Germany (1998–2005) – were pursuing business-friendly policies. Their people wanted economic growth, and supporting global business seemed the best way of achieving that.

Political implications for poor countries

Very few poor countries have working democracies. As far as global business is concerned, however, it doesn't really matter whether a country is democratic. Corporations are happy to do business in India or China, even though the first has a functioning democracy and the second has none at all.

There are ways in which global business helps the spread of democracy in poorer countries. The growth of global media – particularly of the Internet – has spread the idea of democracy and also made it harder for **dictatorships** to keep their people in ignorance. In China, the government has tried to counter the spread of democratic ideas on the Internet by limiting what search engines are allowed to provide.

There are also ways in which global business undermines democracy in poorer countries. The political elites who rule these countries know that they must deal with global business if they are to survive. They create an environment in which global business can prosper. They offer **tax concessions** to global companies, and deal with any local opposition to those companies' plans. In return they prosper. They end up having much more in common with global business people than they have with their own people.

A major political consequence of global business can be war. Some wars are fought over the rights to oil. These two US soldiers are protecting oil pipelines in northern Iraq.

Global business and the environment

In July 2004 two stories appeared in the mainstream US media:

In an article headed "Rise in air travel hurting global environment, study says", *USA Today* reported that: "Rising demand for air travel is one of the most serious environmental risks facing the world, an international research body said. . ."

In an article headed "China, US sign air expansion deal", CNN.com reported that "China and the United States have signed a deal to increase by more than fourfold the number of commercial and cargo flights between the two countries, starting gradually from August. The agreement between the U.S. Department of Transportation and the Civil Aviation Administration of China adds 14 new U.S. passenger flights a week this year and raises the total to 249 flights a week in six years from the current limit of 54."

Despite the worries expressed in the first story, the second story was clearly presented as good news for business. The first story stressed the connection between expanding global business and the environment. The second story ignored the connection altogether. How important is that connection?

As cities develop and grow, so too does the amount of traffic. Vehicles that burn fuels such as petrol and diesel give off harmful fumes into the air, which adds to global warming.

An environment-friendly electric car is tested on a Seattle street in the United States in August 2003. Increased environmental awareness has led to research and development into new, cleaner forms of power.

The global environment

Worries about the global environment have greatly increased over the last 25 years. The signs of trouble are easy to spot. Deserts are spreading, fisheries have fewer fish, water resources are running short, and forests are disappearing. Even the world's climate is changing, as rising **carbon emissions** accelerate the process of **global warming**. Extreme weather events have grown more frequent, and mountain glaciers and Arctic ice caps are melting. Scientists disagree over how fast the process is happening, but most agree that it will be hard – if not impossible – to stop. Some even fear that a "tipping point" could be reached, in which the Earth's climate could take a sudden and dramatic turn for the worse.

Spreading the word

Global business can also play a positive role. The new communication technologies that have opened up the world for business are also being used to spread environmental awareness. In June 2005, BBC News online carried the following article:

"Events have been taking place in more than 100 countries to mark World Environment Day, which is promoting the idea of 'green cities'. The UN estimates that more than 60% of people will live in cities by 2030 . . . This year's World Environment Day has focused on ways of making cities more environmentally friendly and resource-efficient. Events held across the world included a ban on cars in the Greek port of Zakynthos, tree-planting along the tsunami-devastated coastline of Sri Lanka, and a fashion show in Japan encouraging workers to abandon ties and suit jackets, in order to cut air conditioning costs in summer. In San Francisco, mayors from more than 50 cities including Shanghai, Kabul, Sydney and Rome plan to sign up to a scheme setting new green standards for city planning . . . World Environment Day was established by the UN General Assembly in 1972 . . . It is celebrated each year on 5 June."

This hydroelectric power station is on the Rio Conchos near Mexico's northern city of Chihuahua. Many governments are already putting money into renewable energy sources such as this.

Environmental implications for rich countries

Many of the industries that caused pollution in rich countries have been moved to poorer countries, where wages are cheaper and environmental controls are less strict. The generation of energy in the richer countries has also grown more diverse over the last 50 years. The domination of coal and oil has given way to a mix of coal, oil, gas, nuclear energy, and renewable energy (wind, wave, and solar energy). Since nuclear energy and renewable energy are non-carbon-emitting, there has been some reduction in this industry's contribution to global warming. Energy use, by contrast, continues to rise. Car use and air travel are still increasing, and government attempts to reduce carbon emissions are showing little sign of success. If carbon emissions change the climate as some scientists predict, it will affect rich countries as well as poor. Rising sea levels, for example, will submerge parts of coastal cities all over the world.

Individuals, companies, and governments can all reduce their use of carbon-emitting energy. New technologies, such as electric or bio-fuel cars and sail-driven oil tankers, can be developed and promoted. More energy can be saved – and costs therefore reduced – through better insulation of homes and a greater willingness to turn electric appliances off. Road and air journeys can be cut by a greater consumption of products made or grown locally.

As a last resort, however, the people of the world may have to settle for less global business in order to save the environment. This might involve putting less emphasis on making and buying goods, and more emphasis on raising the quality of life in other ways.

Environmental implications for poor countries

The environment has much less protection in poorer countries. Organizations such as the IMF have often insisted that governments cut back on environmental regulation and concentrate on making their countries more "corporate-friendly". Some global businesses, for example the timber business, have done enormous damage to the natural environment of many poorer countries.

The relocation of industries from the rich countries to poorer countries has increased the carbon emissions of those poor countries. In some fast-developing countries, such as China, this increase has combined with greater car use to boost emissions significantly. In Beijing alone, 1,000 cars are added to the roads each day. Generally speaking, however, poorer countries make much smaller contributions to global warming than richer countries.

Will things change?

The current difference between rich and poor countries is likely to continue for several reasons. If all the countries in the world produced carbon emissions at North American and European levels, then global warming would accelerate to the point of environmental collapse. There are also not enough natural resources to support such a level of global economic development. It has been estimated that around 4 hectares (10 acres) of land are needed to provide the average citizen of a rich country with what he or she consumes. Yet, there are only around 1.6 hectares (4 acres) for each person on Earth. Global business cannot increase this amount – it can only provide more natural resources for the richer countries by providing less for the poorer countries.

A global culture?

Business is always about more than just business. Whatever a business is selling – whether it's furniture, energy, food or films – it's also selling a way of life. Global business sells a global way of life: a global culture. It draws everyone together in the same dreams and activities.

There are two sides to this. One argument welcomes global culture as a **melting pot**. For example, this extract from the United Nations Human Development Report, was quoted in the Indian newspaper the *Tribune* in July 2004: "Globalisation has increased contacts between people and their values, ideas and ways of life in unprecedented ways. People are travelling more frequently and more widely. Television now reaches families in the deepest rural areas of China. From Brazilian music in Tokyo to African films in Bangkok, to Shakespeare in Croatia, to books on the history of the Arab world in Moscow, to the CNN world news in Amman, people revel in the diversity of the age of globalisation. For many people this new diversity is exciting, even empowering."

A satellite dish looms over the slums in India's Bangalore, bringing news of "another world".

Globalization has brought aspects of different cultures to different parts of the world. Most cities in the Western world have restaurants that serve traditional foods such as Chinese, Thai, and Japanese cuisine.

"But for some", the report continues, "it is disquieting and disempowering". The other side of the argument stresses the limitations of the melting pot theory. Nearly all the ingredients that count come from the richer countries. Global culture, according to its opponents, is simply the global spread of Western culture. Far from encouraging diversity and difference, it represents the triumph of one set of values and one way of life over all the others.

People such as the Ladakhis, from the Himalayan Mountain region of Ladakh in north-west India, face an agonizing choice between their own traditional way and the Western way, as this article from the *Ecologist* reported in 1999: ". . .as their desire to be 'modern' grows, Ladakhis are turning their backs on their traditional culture. I have seen Ladakhis wearing wristwatches they cannot read, and heard them apologising for the lack of electric lighting in their homes – electric lighting which, in 1975 when it first appeared, most villagers laughed at as an unnecessary gimmick. Even traditional foods are no longer a source of pride: now, when I'm a guest in a Ladakhi village, people apologise if they serve the traditional roasted barley, *ngamphe*, instead of instant noodles. Ironically, then, modernisation – so often associated with the triumph of individualism – has produced a loss of individuality and a growing sense of personal insecurity, as people feel pressured to conform and to live up to an idealised image. By contrast, in the traditional village, where everyone wore essentially the same clothes and looked the same to the casual observer, there was more freedom to relax. As part of a close-knit community, people felt secure enough to be themselves."

The dominance of Western culture

Cultural exports have different sources. The global language of English comes, originally at least, from England. The fast-food culture originated in the United States. The dominant form of popular music comes from both these countries, and is influenced by African and Caribbean music. Many young fashions have started with African-Americans, been adopted by white Americans, and then spread to the rest of the world. Other Western cultural exports – such as increasing equality for women, democratic politics, and the decline of the extended family – have been a feature of all advanced industrial societies.

Most of these cultural exports bring benefits. The rise of a global language could improve communication between peoples. Few would argue with more democracy, and equal rights for the world's women. Even the spread of fast-food outlets offers a wider choice of sorts. The overriding power of one culture and language is, however, bound to weaken others. European leaders have spoken out against the threats that English language poses to their own. "I don't want English to roll over the world like a steamroller, crushing the richness of languages," Swiss interior minister Ruth Dreifuss said in 2000.

In France, campaigns against Anglo-American culture, such as McDonalds, EuroDisney, and the increasing use of English words in common French speech, have been widely supported. Global business has had to adapt to meet the challenge. *Time* magazine carried the following article, headed "Adieu, Ronald McDonald", in January 2004: "Ronald McDonald has been retired as the icon of McDonald's France, replaced by the Gallic nationalist comic-book hero Asterix . . . Americans may find it strange to see their 'official sandwich' touted by a bellicose cartoon warrior with pigtails and a big moustache, but such adjustments are part and parcel of marketing across cultures. Indeed, if an Indian Big Mac tastes a little different, that's because it's a 'lamb-burger' – eating beef offends Hindu tradition. Forget about ordering a cheeseburger at a kosher outlet in Israel (mixing milk and meat is a no-no), but you could always console yourself in Cairo with a 'McFalafel,' or in Bangkok with a 'Samurai Pork Burger.'"

Forced to choose?

In general, rich countries have benefited much more than poorer countries from the cultural side effects of global business. It is their citizens who enjoy the widening choice of products, who listen to the music, and watch the films, and who travel all over the world. It is cities such as London, Paris, and New York that feel like "international cities", and which offer the full range of global culture.

For most people in poorer countries the cultural choice is much more limited. They only have access to two cultures – their own traditional culture and the Western culture that global business brings with it. These two cultures represent such different ways of life that it is almost impossible to combine them. The Western way promises economic development and all the surface excitement of Western culture. It also threatens the traditional place of religion, men, and the elderly.

Some people in poorer countries opt for tradition, and some prefer change. Many of the conflicts that have taken place in poorer countries can be traced to this division: between those who are willing to embrace the dominant global culture and those who are not.

Global tourism is at work here, as a Cook Islander performs a traditional dance for the visiting tourists.

Global education and health care

The rise of global business has had important implications for education and health all over the world. Increasing access to all the various global media – from newspapers to films – has given people a more detailed picture of how people in other countries live. Increased access to the Internet has allowed the free global exchange of information and knowledge. Supporters of global business argue that the greater prosperity such business brings will eventually enable countries to spend more money on their schools and colleges.

Where health matters are concerned, global business offers cause for both hope and concern. If everyone on Earth had access to both Western scientific medicine and old-established traditional medicines (such as those associated with China and India) the benefits would be enormous. At the same time, the huge increase in global flights speeds the spread of new infectious diseases, and gives scientists less time for developing effective vaccines.

Implications for rich countries

Education in rich countries has benefited from global business. Thanks to the Internet and cheap travel, getting access to information and knowledge is much easier than it used to be. Those colleges that provide higher education in rich countries – whether publicly or privately owned – are able to charge high fees to students from poorer countries' elite families. These fees can be used – as they are in some countries – to make the same courses cheaper for students from the home country.

Health and health care have both benefited and suffered from global business. On the positive side, technological improvements and a greater emphasis on health and safety have made many working environments much healthier than they were. Many of the remaining unhealthy jobs are no longer done in the rich countries. The growing practice of traditional Chinese, Ayurvedic, and other traditional medicines in rich countries has given people new options in health care. The rich countries' health and health care industries have gained access to profitable global markets. On the negative side, more travel means that viruses can spread more easily, which increases the chance of global **pandemics**. The need to remain competitive has led many rich countries to reduce their public spending on health care, which has suffered as a result.

An influenza virus, known as "bird flu", is threatening health in many countries around the world. These farmers are wearing masks and protective suits to destroy dead chickens in southern Vietnam.

Chinese medicine

China's experience of global business has been mixed. In the years before the economy was opened to global business wages were extremely low, but health care was free. Over the last 15 years wages have risen for most people, but health care is no longer free. According to BBC News online, an investigation by China's Health Ministry in 2004 highlighted the resulting problems: "The investigation found that 36% of patients in cities and 39% in the countryside did not go to see the doctor because they were unable to afford medical treatment. Nearly 28% of those admitted to hospital left because of economic difficulties."

On a more positive note, global business has accelerated the global spread of traditional Chinese medicine, and not just to rich countries, as this BBC News online reports shows: "Cameroon is gripped by a bitter rivalry between its local doctors and traditional healers from China . . . Almost every town in Cameroon now has at least one traditional Chinese clinic . . . Beatrice Fuh, a locally trained nurse working for a Chinese clinic, says out of 30 patients who visit the clinic every day, only one or two complain of being dissatisfied with the treatment."

Implications for poorer countries

The Internet offers access to a world of knowledge and information, but only to those with computers. Those poorer countries that have done well out of global business have invested some of their profits in education – and computers. Those that have done badly have not been able to do this.

There is now a global market for educational products. These children in Zimbabwe are reading books supplied by a Western publisher.

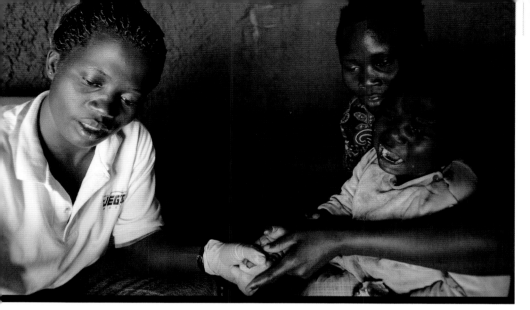

The globalization of medicine should be a positive thing – helping to save lives. This nurse is helping fight AIDS in Uganda.

Western medicines have a huge potential for saving lives in poorer countries, but only if people can afford them. Most cannot, and the drug companies of richer countries have refused to reduce their prices. Pressured by the United States, the World Trade Organization supported drug companies' refusals to allow poorer country manufacturers to copy their medicines. Except, that is, in a "national emergency". The drug companies claim they need high profits to fund future research and development. However, they do little research into the diseases that afflict poorer countries, because most people in those countries cannot afford the drugs. As a result millions die unnecessarily.

Global business has dealt three more blows to the health of the poorer countries. Firstly, importing industries with poor health and safety records from richer countries threatens the health of local people – particularly in the absence of environmental regulations. Secondly, traditional medicines have been squeezed out by Western medicine. In many cases this has more to do with trends in public opinion than with what actually works. For example, many young people in India prefer using expensive antibiotics to treat their colds, rather than the old and tested traditional remedies. Thirdly, many newly trained doctors and nurses are recruited by health businesses in richer countries, where pay and conditions are better. This has led to an acute shortage of health professionals in many poor countries.

Overall, the political elites of poor countries have greatly benefited from the global health care business. Most ordinary people have gained little – and sometimes lost a great deal – from the globalization of health care.

THE PROSPECTS

There is no doubt that the rise of global business has accelerated economic growth. A majority of the world's people have either shared in these new riches or hope to do so in the future. In rich countries most people benefit from global business. Those people who do not benefit are in a minority. In a democracy, this minority does not have the political power to make changes.

In poorer countries only elite minorities benefit. These minorities have usually been willing to use whatever means were necessary to keep themselves in power. In both the richer and poorer countries, those groups that have benefited most from global business hold almost all of the political power.

There does not seem to be an obvious global alternative. Soviet-style communism, which relied on government ownership and control of all large businesses, effectively died out in the 1980s. Social democracy, which relies on regulating and taxing businesses to pay for welfare, is under threat in wealthy countries. This is because their businesses say they need more freedom and more money to compete in the global market. All that remains is neo-liberalism – the belief that global business and free trade will one day benefit everyone.

Concerns about climate change may cause governments to limit the development of global business.

Protecting the environment

The environment has been a major focus of concern for the opponents of global business. The current rate of global economic growth cannot be sustained without using up the planet's resources and drastically altering the planet's climate. In some cases the two are linked. Water, for example, is already in short supply across many parts of the world, but climate change will increase existing demand. Opponents of global business have not been slow to point out such issues.

The quote below comes from an article in the *Independent* in October 2005, headed: "China poses huge threat to global environment":

"According to Lester Brown of the Earth Policy Institute in Washington DC, the leading American environmental analyst, China's scarcely imaginable growth in the coming years means that the world's population will simply run up against the limits of the planet's natural resources sooner than anyone imagines.

"If growth continues at 8 per cent a year, Mr Brown said, by 2031 China's population, likely to be 1.45 billion on current UN predictions, will have an income per person equivalent to that of the US today. He said: 'China's grain consumption will then be two-thirds of the current grain consumption for the entire world. If it consumes oil at the same rate as the US today, the Chinese will be consuming 99 billion barrels a day, and the whole world is currently producing 84 million barrels a day, and will probably not produce much more. If it consumes paper at the same rate we do, it will consume twice as much paper as the world is now producing. There go the world's forests. If the Chinese then have three cars for every four people – as the US does today – they would have a fleet of 1.1 billion cars, compared to the current world fleet of 800 million. They would have to pave over an area equivalent to the area they have planted with rice today, just to drive and park them …

"'The Western economic model is not going to work for China. All they're doing is what we've already done, so you can't criticise them for that. But what you can say is, it's not going to work.'"

Ignoring environmental threats

Despite the concerns that have been raised, global business has mostly chosen to ignore the threat it poses to the environment. Governments have been either unwilling or unable to make them take notice. Those who take decisions in corporate boardrooms and government offices are – understandably – more worried about next year's profits and next year's elections than the state of the planet in 2050. The needs of the environment should be limiting the freedom of global business, but limiting it would result in slower economic growth and a reduction of prosperity for many. Very few politicians have been willing to argue for the unpopular measures that are clearly necessary. Future generations may have to pay the price for the present generation's recklessness.

The unofficial opposition

Since most mainstream political parties have generally supported global business, most opposition has come from unofficial groups and organizations. Some of these groups are small, but others – such as the environmental group Greenpeace – have been every bit as global as the transnational corporations. These groups and organizations represent small farmers, trade unionists, pacifists, animal rights campaigners, environmentalists, and believers in many other causes. Each group has its own favourite issue, but all are linked by what they see as their common enemy: global business. Together, these groups and organizations make up the "anti-globalization movement".

Over the last decade the anti-globalization movement has mounted a series of large protests. They have focused on political summits (meetings of **G8**, **NAFTA**, and EU leaders) and meetings of the international financial institutions (the WTO, IMF, and World Bank). The protests at the WTO meeting in Seattle, USA, in 1999 and at the G8 summit in Genoa, Italy, in 2001 attracted many people, and were given wide coverage in the media. The coverage of such events, however, has frequently been biased against the protesters. Take this report from the *Observer* on the 2005 WTO conference in Hong Kong for example: "Police used water cannon, tear gas and pepper spray to repulse protesters – mostly Korean farmers – who tried to break through their lines with iron bars, wooden poles and battering rams made from steel security barriers. With the clashes spread out over several hours and locations, there were numerous injuries, including several Koreans and police with bloody head wounds, and a woman who lost consciousness amid a thick, acrid cloud of tear gas."

The article went on to describe "grim-faced riot police", "ambulance sirens", and the "buzz of police helicopters". In the entire report only two paragraphs explained the reasons behind the protests. The writers may have thought that most of their readers would be more interested in street violence than the details of trade deals, and they may have been right.

This is what the article had to say on the reasons behind the protest: "The demonstrators' anger has been stirred up by reports that negotiators are moving closer to a compromise package that does not include the key demand of many NGOs (non-governmental organizations): an end to European and American agriculture subsidies that are destroying the livelihood of farmers in poor countries."

Americans protest against rising fuel prices in a rally in Washington DC. High US fuel consumption is believed to be a major cause of global warming.

Fairtrade logos tell shoppers in Western supermarkets that the farmers were given a fair price for their produce.

Debt cancellation and "Fairtrade"

Opponents of unrestricted global business have also proposed ways of softening its harmful impact on the poorest countries and individuals. Many poorer countries borrowed large sums of money over the last 25 years of the 20th century, and over the last 10 years there has been increasing pressure from campaigning groups to reduce or cancel these debts. Some have been cancelled, but many others remain.

The spread of Fairtrade goods has also helped many people in poorer countries. Traditionally, a coffee farmer, for example, would sell his crop to a local buyer, who would then sell the crop on to a Western coffee company at a higher price. Under the Fairtrade system the local buyer is left out and the consumer in a wealthy country agrees to pay a higher price. This leaves more money for the farmer. If all people in richer countries were prepared to pay a higher price for all their goods, global business would be fairer for many people in poorer countries.

A worrying future

Global business in the early 21st century has many similarities with British, American, and German business in the late 19th century. The 19th-century system was also enormously productive, creating wealth at an almost dizzying speed. It also created a widening gap between rich and poor, and led to the same accusations of unfairness that global business faces today.

In the 19th century the business system supplied its own answer – the freedom that encouraged business also encouraged democracy. People formed trade unions and political parties that campaigned for a narrowing of the gap between rich and poor, and for the introduction of welfare benefits such as pensions and unemployment pay. Business kept growing, but a little slower. Some of the growth was sacrificed for greater fairness.

Will global business be forced into the same sacrifice? Public pressure, whether exerted through media exposure or **consumer boycotts**, can be effective. However, there are no global political parties or unions, and there is no global government. Those who suffer from global business can put pressure on their own governments, but these are often powerless to alter the behaviour of the transnational corporations. In the short term, at least, there are no obvious limits to the continuing growth of global business.

Solar panels donated by an international charity organization form part of an agricultural project in the Gambia.

Who benefits from global business?

Deciding who benefits from global business is not a simple matter. There are millions of outright winners and many more outright losers, but most people both benefit and suffer from the system. They benefit from the wealth the system creates, and they suffer from the damage it does to the planet. Some are more inclined to stress the benefits, and others to stress the cost.

Some are happy to take what they can, while others are more concerned with making the system fairer.

A march of protesters in downtown Hong Kong during the World Trade Organization meeting of December 2005.

Think about the following:

- What benefits has global business brought to humanity as a whole?
- Does global business share its benefits evenly? Could everybody benefit, or does global business, by its very nature, create a widening gap between the rich and the poor?
- Who has suffered from the spread of global business?
- How have governments and international organizations helped global business, and why?
- Do the media pay enough attention to global business? Has their reporting been accurate and unbiased?
- Can the planet cope with continuing economic growth at the current rate, and if not, what are the alternatives?

The south Shanghai skyline is a symbol of global business growth. In the early 1990s the area pictured here was farmland.

How would you answer these questions? Can you find additional information in other publications to support your views or to change them?

It seems certain that global business will continue to grow, and that those who benefit from it will continue to do so. Two big questions remain:
- Can the benefits of global business be made available to everyone?
- Could the environment stand the strain if they were?

Anyone who goes into a shop is already making some decisions about global business. Buying flowers on a winter's day, for example, means saying yes to the flights that bring them in from sunnier places. At the same time, it also means saying yes to jobs in those hotter, and often poorer, countries. Buying the cheapest goods often means supporting the movement of jobs to countries where labour is cheap. However, the living standards of at least some people in that country will be raised.

One day you might have to make more important decisions about global business. You might be voting in an election, or speaking in a debate. You might be a journalist, a politician, or a salesperson for a global corporation. How will you use the media to learn about news and events? Will you know how to find out which news and information is accurate and free of one-sided opinions? Will you hear and respect opposing views?

One thing is certain – there is no escape from global business and the world it continues to remake. How we deal with it will determine what sort of planet we have, and what sort of lives we can live on it.

This table shows the approximate Gross Domestic Product (GDP) of the world's top 18 nations in 2005, compared to World and European Union GDP. There are several ways of calculating GDP and it is very difficult to get consistent information about production from every country in the world. These figures are estimates.

Gross Domestic Product	(billions of US$)	Gross Domestic Product	(billions of US$)
World	59,590	Brazil	1,568
United States	12,410	Russia	1,539
European Union	12,180	Canada	1,080
China	8,182	Mexico	1,068
Japan	3,914	Spain	1,017
India	3,699	South Korea	965
Germany	2,454	Indonesia	902
United Kingdom	1,869	Australia	642
France	1,822	Taiwan	612
Italy	1,651	Iran	553

2005 estimates

WORLD GDP

This graph shows the growth of the world's Gross Domestic Product in recent years. Much of this growth is due to the increased globalization of business.

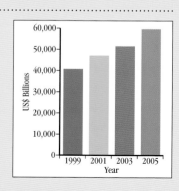

This table compares the 2004 revenues of the 10 leading global corporations with the approximate 2005 Gross Domestic Product (GDP) of some nations. Many economists would not compare nations' GDP with corporation revenue because they do not show the same thing, and make corporations look more powerful than they are. But the figures do give some idea of how large corporations can be.

Nation or corporation	(billions of US$)	Nation or corporation	(billions of US$)
Belgium	331	Romania	187
Wal-Mart Stores	288	Czech Republic	186
BP	285	Daimler/Chrysler	177
Exxon Mobil	271	Toyota Motor	173
Austria	270	Ford Motor	172
Royal Dutch/Shell Group	269	Peru	170
Sweden	268	Finland	160
Switzerland	264	General Electric	153
Malaysia	249	Total	153
Portugal	196	Israel	140
Norway	195	Singapore	132
General Motors	194		

WORLD EXPORTS

This graph shows the growth of the world's export trade in recent years. It helps to show that there has been an increased globalization of business.

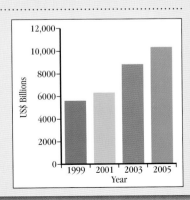

GLOSSARY

bias for or against a particular viewpoint. For example, an article can be biased towards a particular political party.

biotechnology use of biological processes for industrial purposes

carbon emissions releases of carbon dioxide into the atmosphere, usually as a result of burning carbon-based fuels such as coal, oil, or gas

communism political theory that puts the interests of society as a whole above the interests of individuals

Congress political party in India

consumer boycott refusal to buy the products of certain corporations

corporation large company, often made up of several smaller companies working together

democracy political system in which governments are regularly elected by the mass of the people

democratic responding to the wishes of all those concerned

dictatorship country ruled by a person who has complete power and authority

domestic market buying and selling within one country

economy all the activities concerned with the making, distribution, and consumption of goods and services

editorial article, or opinion piece, where the writer or editor expresses their own opinion on an issue

elite most wealthy, powerful, or gifted members of a group

environmentalist someone who campaigns to protect the planet's environment

environmental regulations rules designed to protect the environment

European Union (EU) economic and political organization made up of many European countries

export revenue amount of money a country makes from selling goods and services to other countries

free enterprise capitalism form of economic and political organization that relies on individuals – and not governments – taking decisions about what is bought and sold

free trade trade between countries that is free from most legal and financial restrictions

G8 group of the eight leading industrial countries: United States, Germany, Japan, United Kingdom, France, Italy, Canada, and Russia

GDP (Gross Domestic Product) sum total of everything a country produces in a year

General Agreement on Tariffs and Trade (GATT) predecessor of the World Trade Organization (WTO)

genetically modified (GM) altered at the genetic level, through manipulation of an organism's DNA

global warming gradual warming of Earth's atmosphere, which is mostly caused by rising levels of carbon dioxide

health benefits payments made by companies or governments to help people get medical treatment and improve their health

interest extra amount charged when repaying a loan

International Monetary Fund (IMF) organization set up in 1946 to regulate international money matters

left (also called left-wing) usually, radical or reforming parties that believe governments should take a large role in reforming society and running economies

market reforms changes that ease the workings of a free market

mass campaigning movements movements made up of ordinary people who share a political aim

melting pot phrase used to describe different people and cultures coming together in one place

multinational involving several countries

NAFTA North American Free Trade Association, which includes Canada, the United States, and Mexico

neo-liberalism belief that a global free market and global free trade are in everyone's long-term interests

pandemics illnesses that spread around the world

per capita income money earned by each person

privatize sell something that is owned by the government to private individuals

protectionism use of tariffs (charges for bringing goods across international borders) to protect industry and agriculture from foreign competition

right (also called right-wing) usually, political parties that do not want major reforms to society, or want to return to traditional ways. Right-wing parties usually support free enterprise capitalism.

significant minority important part of a group, even though it is less than half of the group

socio-economic relating to both social and economic factors

subsidiary smaller company owned by a larger company

subsidy/subsidize extra money given, usually by a government, to help out individuals or businesses

tax concessions reductions in the amount of tax that needs to be paid

trade barrier anything that stops the free movement of goods

trade union organization formed to protect and advance the pay and conditions of workers

transnational operating internationally – across national borders

welfare financial support given to those who, through no fault of their own, are unable to support themselves

World Bank international bank set up in 1946 to help promote economic development. Its official name is the International Bank for Reconstruction and Development.

World Trade Organization (WTO) successor to General Agreement on Tariffs and Trade (GATT) set up in 1995. Its role is to regulate world trade.

FIND OUT MORE

Globalisation, Rob Bowden (Hodder Wayland, 2003)

Globalisation, Iris Teichmann (Franklin Watts, 2002)

Planet Under Pressure: Energy, Clive Gifford (Raintree, 2005)

A Citizen's Guide to the World Community, Sean Connolly (Heinemann Library, 2006)

Books for older readers
Globalization and its Discontents, Joseph Stiglitz (W. W. Norton, 2002)

In Defense of Globalization, Jagdish Bhagwati (Oxford University Press, 2004)

No Logo, Naomi Klein (Flamingo, 2001)

The No-Nonsense Guide to Globalization, Wayne Ellwood (New Internationalist/Verso, 2001)

The Silent Takeover, Noreena Hertz (William Heinemann, 2001)

Websites
News websites
CNN
www.cnn.com

BBC
www.bbcworld.com

New York Times
www.nytimes.com

The Guardian
www.guardian.co.uk

The Economist
www.economist.com

New Internationalist
www.newint.org

Websites of international organizations

World Trade Organization (WTO)
www.wto.org

International Monetary Fund
www.imf.org

United Nations
www.un.org

Friends of the Earth
www.foe.org

International Forum on Globalization
www.ifg.org

Corporate Watch
www.corporatewatch.org.uk

Greenpeace
www.greenpeace.org

Activities

Here are some ideas for finding out more about global business.

- Have a look at some things you have bought, and at cars, mobile phones, and personal computers. Which companies made them? Could you buy the same things in another country?

- Look at the foods you eat, the clothes you wear, and other things around your home. Were they made or grown in your country? Who made or grew them?

- Choose a global corporation and find out how many people it employs around the world. How many countries does it have offices and factories in? Is it made up of many smaller companies? Do they all make or sell the same products?